Roy Floyd's Shoes

by Susan Mihalic
illustrations by Thom Ricks

Harcourt Brace & Company

Orlando Atlanta Austin Boston San Francisco Chicago Dallas New York Toronto London

Roy Floyd's shoes made noise.
"That noise is annoying,"
said Joyce.

"Roy Floyd," said Mom, "that annoying noise gives me no joy."

Roy Floyd soiled his shoes to stop the noise. Roy Floyd's soiled shoes still made noise.

Roy Floyd oiled his shoes to stop the noise. Roy Floyd's oiled shoes made more noise.

Roy Floyd boiled his shoes to stop the noise. Roy Floyd's boiled shoes were moist, but they still made noise.

Roy broiled his shoes to stop the noise. Roy Floyd's broiled shoes were crisp, and they made LOTS of noise.

Roy Floyd had no choice. He gave up and joined his toys. The noise didn't annoy Cowboy Troy.

But Mom was annoyed. Joyce
was annoyed. Even Roy Floyd
was annoyed.

"Roy Floyd," Mom said, pointing, "your shoes were soiled, oiled, boiled, and broiled. But boy-oh-boy, they still make noise."

Mom gave Roy Floyd a box.
"Roy Floyd," she said, "here are
shoes we can all enjoy."

"These shoes aren't soiled, oiled, boiled, or broiled!" said Roy Floyd. "Best of all, they don't make NOISE!"